A
Short and Sweet Introduction

to

Indianapolis

a travel guide for Indianapolis

Joe Dodridge
©2018

A Short and Sweet Introduction to Indianapolis: a travel guide for Indianapolis

1st edition

www.shortandsweetintroductions.com

Copyright ©2018
ISBN: 978-0-692-14475-6

Table of Contents

PLANNING YOUR TRIP

EVERYTHING ELSE

SPECIAL TIP!!!

Visit

www.shortandsweetintroductions.com/indylinks

for links to all of the websites, books, and other
resources referred to throughout this book.

Why an Indianapolis Guide Book?

Try to find an updated Indianapolis guide book. I dare you.

You will find a few books on things to do – like where to eat. There are maps and pictorials and calendars and journals. There are books about ghosts and trains and where to take a hike (not that kind of "take a hike").

But, when it comes to a normal guide about Indianapolis, they are hard to find. The best-known one was published in 2010 (2010!!!). A lot has changed since 2010.

A Short and Sweet Introduction to Indianapolis is your guide to everything you need to know to start your visit to Indianapolis. What are the major attractions? Where are the cool neighborhoods? What will my kids like?

When I introduce myself to someone, I give them my name, what I do, and where I live. I'll also talk about my wife and kids. I don't tell them everything about me, like the details of my last doctor's appointment, my political preferences, or the status of my bank accounts.

That's what this book is – an introduction to Indianapolis.

This book isn't going to review every hotel and restaurant in Indianapolis. That's not what an introduction is (that's what the Internet is for!). I'll throw in a few tips and tricks along the way and give you what you need to know.

So, I'd like to introduce you to Indianapolis. Not an introduction from 2010, but one from today. And definitely not an Indianapolis encyclopedia, just an introduction.

Indianapolis in Two Pages

I've visited a lot of cities in the United States and I have to admit that Indianapolis stands heads and shoulders above most. Alive, walkable, and exciting all describe Indianapolis.

When people say Indianapolis is walkable, they don't mean it is necessarily small. Rather, the downtown core of Indianapolis is easy to navigate, has a ton to do, and is busy just about any night you visit.

Every year 25-30 million people visit Indianapolis, putting it in the top 25 visited cities of the United States.

Downtown, there are over 7000 hotel rooms with more being built. The downtown convention center (one of the 20 largest in the United States) is connected by skywalks to more hotel rooms than any convention center in any other city in the United States. Downtown there is a four-story mall (also connected by the skywalks) and three large sports stadiums.

Downtown has great museums, about 200 restaurants and clubs, bike trails, a canal you can actually take a gondola on, the most war memorials of any city except Washington DC, and an awesome zoo.

Tired of walking yet?

Outside of downtown is the largest children's museum IN THE WORLD, a large art museum, eclectic neighborhoods, shopping, dining, and lodging.

And, oh yeah, one more little thing – Indianapolis has the INDIANAPOLIS MOTOR SPEEDWAY, home of the Indy 500!

Indianapolis is home to the Indianapolis Colts (NFL), Indiana Pacers (NBA) and the Indiana Fever (WNBA). It is also home to the minor league teams Indianapolis Indians (baseball), Indy Eleven (soccer), and Indy Fuel (hockey).

Actually, professional sports might only be half of the Indianapolis sports picture. Indianapolis is home to the NCAA national headquarters, including an NCAA museum. Indianapolis is home to Butler University and IUPUI, both playing Division I basketball. But, more than all of this, Indianapolis regularly hosts large sporting events, including the Super Bowl, NCAA basketball Final Four and regional championships, Big Ten football and basketball championships, Olympic qualifiers, other collegiate championships, and other professional championships.

IUPUI (Indiana University-Purdue University of Indianapolis) is adjacent to downtown. Outside of the metro area, Indiana University, Purdue University, Ball State University, and Indiana State University are each about an hour's drive from Indianapolis.

Interested in shopping? There's a big mall downtown and the biggest mall in Indiana just on the edge of Indianapolis. There are also quaint neighborhoods inside and outside of Indianapolis with restaurants and shops.

Outside of the metro you can take a shot on the floor of Hoosier Gym where the movie *Hoosiers* was filmed. Or, you can hike in Brown County, known as the "Little Smokies."

There's a lot to Indianapolis – it's a great place to live and to visit.

Maps

Indianapolis Metro Area

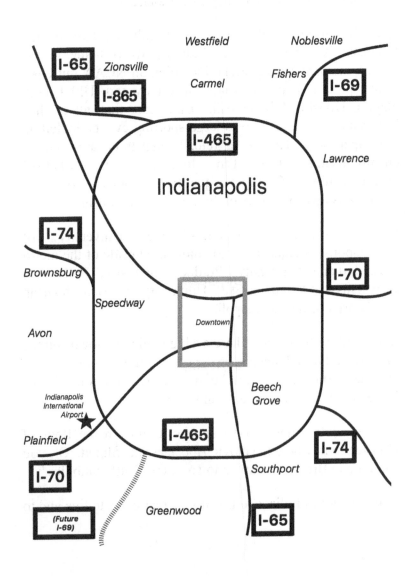

Downtown

(the numbers correspond to book page number and map key)

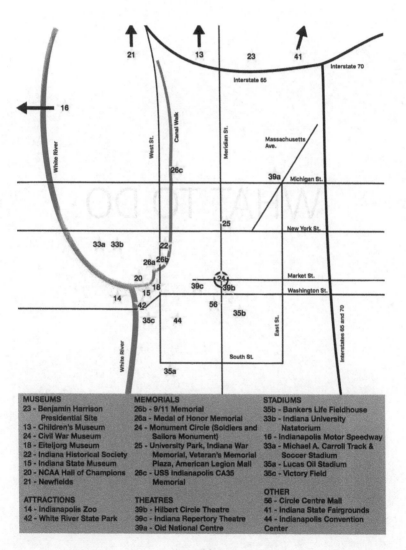

MUSEUMS
23 - Benjamin Harrison
     Presidential Site
13 - Children's Museum
24 - Civil War Museum
18 - Eiteljorg Museum
22 - Indiana Historical Society
15 - Indiana State Museum
20 - NCAA Hall of Champions
21 - Newfields

ATTRACTIONS
14 - Indianapolis Zoo
42 - White River State Park

MEMORIALS
26b - 9/11 Memorial
26a - Medal of Honor Memorial
24 - Monument Circle (Soldiers and
     Sailors Monument)
25 - University Park, Indiana War
     Memorial, Veteran's Memorial
     Plaza, American Legion Mall
26c - USS Indianapolis CA35
     Memorial

THEATRES
39b - Hilbert Circle Theatre
39c - Indiana Repertory Theatre
39a - Old National Centre

STADIUMS
35b - Bankers Life Fieldhouse
33b - Indiana University
     Natatorium
16 - Indianapolis Motor Speedway
33a - Michael A. Carroll Track &
     Soccer Stadium
35a - Lucas Oil Stadium
35c - Victory Field

OTHER
56 - Circle Centre Mall
41 - Indiana State Fairgrounds
44 - Indianapolis Convention
     Center

11

WHAT TO DO

Museums, Monuments, and Attractions

Children's Museum of Indianapolis

This is the biggest children's museum in the world! Located just a few miles north of downtown, the Children's Museum is a must-see for anyone traveling with children.

Five stories tall, the museum boasts several permanent exhibits, including life-size dinosaurs complete with real paleontologists working on real fossils! You can interact with science exhibits, take a trip to China, climb through a real steam train, visit the International Space Station, and even watch a play.

New in 2018, children can play outside in a massive, 7.5-acre sports exhibit. And, if you're traveling to Indianapolis around Christmas, make sure to visit the Children's Museum for its popular holiday activities.

Ticket prices vary based on the day you plan to attend, though you can always purchase tickets online in advance cheaper than buying them the day you attend. Children under two are free, and they offer memberships for frequent attenders!

The Children's Museum closes most days at 5:00PM; be sure you plan so that your children can play for a couple of hours. There is a large cafeteria at the Children's Museum. Parking is free and you can also take IndyGo to get to the museum.

Indianapolis Zoo

Located in White River State Park, the Indianapolis Zoo presents animals in neat exhibits, with a premium placed on interacting with the animals. Popular exhibits include:

*Oceans where you can pet sharks (for real!) and watch penguins play. You can also watch a dolphin show and learn more about conservation.
*Orangutan Center where you can watch these amazing creatures interact with each other and maybe even with you!
*Flights of Fancy where you can walk through an aviary and feed the birds.
*Deserts where you enter into a warm desert environment inhabited by snakes, meerkats, lizards, and turtles.

Of course, you can also see elephants, cheetahs, bears, giraffes, zebras, and more.

Admission prices to the zoo vary, based on the day you choose to attend. Advance tickets are cheaper than day-of tickets. Additionally, there are discounts for current and former military members, AAA members, and members of certain other zoos. Unfortunately, you have to pay for parking, though you can walk to the zoo through White River State Park – the zoo is about a one-mile, safe walk from most of downtown.

Admission gets you access to both the zoo and the White River Gardens. Other attractions cost extra, such as riding the train, feeding the birds, and racing a cheetah (sort of). There are plenty of food options at the zoo and while you can't bring in food, you can exit the zoo to eat your own food in an outdoor picnic area next to the parking lot.

Indiana State Museum

Located in White River State Park along the Canal Walk, the Indiana State Museum holds exhibits all about Indiana – its culture, history, and achievements. With exhibits geared to adults and children alike, it is easy to spend a couple of hours exploring the museum.

Of course, you need to allow yourself more time if you take in a movie. The Indiana State Museum has the largest IMAX movie screen in the state. Playing both educational and blockbuster films, the museum's IMAX theater has movie times throughout the day and evening – even after the museum has closed.

Museum admission prices do not vary throughout the year, but you can save a little money if you purchase museum tickets in advance online. You can also save money on your museum admission if you purchase IMAX tickets. In addition, the Indiana State Museum is a member of the Association of Science-Technology Centers. That means that if you have a pass to one of the reciprocal museums, your admission to the Indiana State Museum might be free! (There are residency and home membership exclusions – see the ASTC website for details.)

Parking is conveniently located in the White River State Park underground garage, which is connected to the Indiana State Museum. You even get a parking discount if you purchase museum tickets or make a minimum purchase in the museum's gift store or cafe. Furthermore, parking is free if you purchase an IMAX ticket.

The Indiana State Museum does have a cafe (full service is only available for lunch) and a museum gift store – the perfect place to find Indiana-specific souvenirs.

Indianapolis Motor Speedway Museum

Located a 15-minute drive from downtown, the Indianapolis Motor Speedway Museum celebrates not just Indy racing, but automobiles and automobile racing in general.

The museum is located in the infield of the Indianapolis Motor Speedway. One of the neatest experiences when visiting the museum is driving through the tunnel under the racetrack, and then out into the infield.

The museum itself might focus on Indy cars (and has a collection of former Indy 500 winning cars), but it also has NASCAR cars, Formula One cars, midget cars, and dragsters. And, since racing focuses on speed, the museum houses record-holding land speed vehicles. The museum does have two gift shops, but no dining.

Just as neat as the museum are the tours you can take of the speedway. The shortest (and cheapest) tour –Track Laps – is a narrated tour that takes one lap around the 2½ mile track. And, although you're not cruising at a breakneck speed, it is still spine-tingling to ride down the final stretch and across its famous bricks. Other tours are available; see the museum's website for more details.

Tour fees are independent of museum admission fees. Adults and children are separate prices, while children 5 and under are free.

Parking is free (and thus admission to drive your car into the infield is free) unless there is a track event. In that case, to go to the museum you will need a ticket to that day's event. You should not expect to be able to park in the infield on event days, even if your primary purpose is to visit the museum.

While not part of the museum, the Indianapolis Motor Speedway also hosts the Richard Petty Driving Experience, where you can ride along or even drive race cars on the speedway.

Eiteljorg Museum of American Indians and Western Art

With a focus on the culture of both American Indians and people of the great out west, the Eiteljorg Museum of American Indians and Western Art is located in White River State Park, adjacent to the Canal Walk and next to the Indiana State Museum. Containing weapons, baskets, pottery, clothing, sculpture, jewelry, paintings, and other artifacts and art work, the Eiteljorg consists of galleries and some interactive exhibits.

Aside from the regular exhibits, the Eiteljorg hosts artists in residence who give scheduled talks. There are also frequent festivals and art markets where you can purchase American Indian and western art-inspired goods. And, if you are in town at Christmas, the Eiteljorg's yearly holiday exhibit, Jingle Rails, shows model trains traversing from a model of modern-day Indianapolis westward through famous western-American scenes.

While the Eiteljorg has standard admission prices (regardless of the day you plan to attend or advance purchase), they also offer several discounts and even free admission. While you should check their website for more details, free admission is available for Native Americans, Indiana school teachers, and IUPUI students and staff. There are also several reciprocal agreements with various museum organizations. In addition, the Eiteljorg offers discounted tickets for AAA members, active duty military members, convention attendees and downtown hotel guests.

If you're hungry, the Eiteljorg has a lunchtime cafeteria serving a variety of food, including food that focuses on the American southwest. The Frank and Katrina Basile Museum

18

Store carries a variety of American Indian and western gifts, jewelry, and other items. If you drive, you can park in the White River State Park garage for free if you pay for admission to the Eiteljorg.

NCAA Hall of Champions

The NCAA Hall of Champions is the official interactive museum of NCAA collegiate athletics. Built in 2000 after the NCAA moved their headquarters to Indianapolis, the museum boasts two floors that celebrate the history of all 24 sports sanctioned by the National Collegiate Athletic Association.

In addition to celebrating history and showcasing collegiate artifacts, the museum has interactive areas where visitors can shoot a basketball and participate in other sports virtually and in real life. Besides regular exhibits, the museum houses temporary exhibits and events throughout the year.

Partly due to the NCAA Hall of Champions connection to the NCAA headquarters, the museum also boasts event space for both small meetings and large banquets and presentations. With its own caterer, the Hall of Champions can accommodate several hundred guests.

Located adjacent to the White River State Park and on the Canal Walk, the NCAA Hall of Champions shares a parking garage with the Indiana State Museum and the Eiteljorg Museum. However, if you are staying downtown, you will most likely want to walk to the museum.

Admission to the NCAA Hall of Champions costs different for adults and children. In addition, children 5 and under are free. There is no cafeteria in the museum, but there is a gift shop where you can buy officially licensed NCAA merchandise.

Note that the NCAA Hall of Champions is closed most Mondays throughout the year and also some Tuesdays. Visit their website for details.

Newfields (Indianapolis Museum of Art)

Making a bold change in 2017, the Indianapolis Museum of Art adopted the name Newfields in an attempt to focus on their entire experience, which includes grounds, houses, the art museum, and other events and activities.

Part of Newfields, the **Indianapolis Museum of Art** contains over 50,000 works and is one of the largest and oldest such museums in the United States. The museum contains paintings, sculptures, photography, textiles, drawings, and fashion from all over the world, covering multiple millennia. The museum boasts a cafe and a gift shop.

The **Lilly House** is a National Historic Landmark and the large mansion of former Indianapolis resident, J.K. Lilly, Jr. You can explore the rooms which are restored to the 1930s.

The **Virginia B. Banks Art and Nature Park** is a 100-acre outdoor area of woods, water, and wetlands that celebrates nature.

The **Garden** is a 50-acre collection of gardens featuring flowers, plants, and trees, with weaving walkways.

The **Elder Greenhouse** is a fully restored and functioning greenhouse.

Newfields is located about 15 minutes northwest of downtown Indy and has free parking. It is open Tuesday through Sunday year-round. There is an admission charge – with separate prices for adults and children, though admission to most outdoor areas is free.

Indiana Historical Society

Located downtown on the canal, the Indiana Historical Society tells the story of Indiana's history. It is the oldest historical society outside of the east coast and maintains records not just on Indiana's history as a state, but also the Midwest's history when it was America's frontier.

The Indiana Historical Society functions as both an interactive museum and research library. The You Are There exhibits use character actors who help immerse you into the stories they are telling. Destination Indiana tells stories from each corner of the state, covering all 92 counties. And, you can listen to a Cole Porter impersonator sing the Indiana native's popular songs.

Aside from interactive exhibits, the Indiana Historical Society contains artwork, manuscripts, maps, sheet music, artifacts, and countless other items. In addition to housing thousands of items, the society also publishes books and magazines throughout the year.

Admission pricing is different for adults, seniors, and children (children under 5 are free). The museum is open year-round, but is closed on Sundays and Mondays. The museum has a cafe of soups, salads, sandwiches and wraps. They also offer some breakfast items all day long and they have a kids menu. In addition, the Indiana Historical Society has a gift shop full of both Indiana souvenirs and Indiana history items.

Benjamin Harrison Presidential Site

Hoosier native Benjamin Harrison was the 23rd President of the United States. The grandson of President William Henry Harrison, Benjamin Harrison grew up in Ohio, but moved with his wife to Indianapolis a couple of years after he graduated college. A lawyer by education and practice, Benjamin Harrison was elected to the United States Senate and then one term as President of the United States from 1889-1893.

The Benjamin Harrison Presidential Site is located just north of downtown Indy. It consists of the 16-room house and the surrounding gardens that Harrison built in 1874 and lived in until his death in 1901. The museum includes artifacts from Benjamin Harrison's life and presidency, temporary exhibits that change from year to year, artwork, photographs, a research library, various events, and outdoor gardens.

The museum is open most days year-round, Monday through Saturdays (and Sundays during some summer months). Tours last approximately one hour and fifteen minutes and there is an admission cost (children, seniors, and AAA members get discounts).

In addition to the museum exhibits, the Benjamin Harrison Presidential Site contains a gift shop of various artifacts and books, as well as souvenirs. Parking is free, though limited (you might be able to park on the street for free if the lot is full).

Monument Circle

Soldiers and Sailors Monument

Built in 1902 to memorialize Indiana's Civil War veterans, the Soldiers and Sailors Monument stands 284 feet tall in the center of Indianapolis – right in the middle of Monument Circle. Television sports broadcasts almost always include a picture of the Soldiers and Sailors Monument. Recently the TV show "American Ninja Warrior" constructed its first-ever curved obstacle course around the monument.

The monument has a small gift shop inside as well as an elevator and stairway that lets you go to the top. Providing the best public view of Indianapolis, the observation deck is 275 feet off the ground and offers views each direction out of the top of the monument.

The monument is generally open Wednesday through Sunday during warmer months and only Friday through Sunday during colder months. It is free to walk up the stairs but costs a small fee to use the elevator. Please note that even if you pay to use the elevator, you will have to climb a small number of steps at the top. Also note that the monument gets tighter as you go up and might not be ideal for people who don't like small spaces.

Colonel Eli Lilly Civil War Museum

This museum is located in the bottom level of the Soldiers and Sailors Monument. Its entrance is on the west side (while the monument's observation entrance is on the south side). The Colonel Eli Lilly Civil War Museum hosts 9000 square feet of artifacts from the Civil War. Admission to the museum is free and usually has the same hours as the Soldiers and Sailors Monument.

Other War Memorials

Indianapolis has more war memorials than any other city in the United States except Washington DC. University Park, the Indiana War Memorial, Veteran's Memorial Plaza, and the American Legion Mall are located in a row extending in a straight line one block north of Monument Circle. The Medal of Honor Memorial, 9/11 Memorial, and USS Indianapolis CA35 Memorial, are located along the canal.

University Park

Originally land intended to be a state university, University Park contains monuments of famous Hoosiers who had a national impact. Benjamin Harrison was Indiana's only president. Abraham Lincoln grew up in Indiana. Schuyler Colfax was vice president to Ulysses S. Grant.

Indiana War Memorial

Built to honor Indiana veterans of World War I, the Indiana War Memorial honors Hoosiers who have served in all wars, conflicts, and peacekeeping missions. Inside the memorial is the Indiana War Museum which has thousands of historic and modern military artifacts, a unique battle flag collection of over 400 flags, and the Shrine Room which is full of objects commemorating World War I. Museum admission is free and is open Wednesday through Sunday during the day.

Veteran's Memorial Plaza

Veteran's Memorial Plaza is anchored by an obelisk and part of a large green space that is used for festivals and special events. The obelisk is similar to the Washington Monument in Washington DC (though much smaller and without the ability to go inside of it). Veteran's Memorial Plaza honors all fifty states with their flags.

American Legion Mall

This green space is so named because the American Legion's national headquarters sits on one side while the American Legion's Indiana headquarters sits on the other side. Within the green space are small memorials for World War II, the Korean War, and the Vietnam War, as well as Cenotaph Square (which memorializes the first U.S. life lost in World War I). Each memorial lists the names of Hoosiers who died in those wars.

Medal of Honor Memorial

Sitting right beside the canal (near the Indiana State Museum), the Medal of Honor Memorial is the only memorial in the United States that lists and honors all recipients of the U.S. Medal of Honor. The glass memorial is lit at night and has a motion-activated recording that plays, telling the stories of some of the recipients.

9/11 Memorial

Containing two steel beams from the World Trade Center, the 9/11 Memorial remembers the attack on 9/11. In addition to the beams are two black granite walls that observe the attack. The 9/11 Memorial is located along the canal a block east of the Medal of Honor Memorial.

USS Indianapolis CA35 Memorial

Sunk by a Japanese submarine in 1945 and recently memorialized in a movie starring Nicolas Cage, the USS Indianapolis delivered critical atomic bomb parts in World War II shortly before it sank. Most of the men aboard the ship died and this memorial (located at the north end of the canal) honors their loss.

Sports

Racing

Racing has been synonymous with Indianapolis for over 100 years. Surrounding Indianapolis, you will find auto racing, bicycle racing, airplane racing, motorcycle racing, and drag racing.

The Indianapolis 500 is the king of all races in Indianapolis. The Indy 500 is not just a single-day event, but rather a month-long celebration called the 500 Festival. There is a huge, televised parade, one of the largest half-marathons in the world, the exclusive Snakepit Ball, and everything that has to do with the actual race. For two weeks, people in Indy attend practice days, qualification day, pole day, carb day, and legends day – all before the actual race day!

The Indianapolis Motor Speedway hosts the Indianapolis 500 (IndyCar), the Brickyard 400 (NASCAR), IndyCar Grand Prix, Vintage Racing, and Air Racing. The Indianapolis Motor Speedway has also hosted MotoGP in the past.

Lucas Oil Raceway (Crawfordsville – 30 minutes west of downtown) has a drag strip, oval track, and road course. The raceway hosts a variety of local and national races from March through October.

The Indianapolis Speedrome (20 minutes east of downtown Indy) is considered the oldest figure-8 racetrack in the United States. The track hosts a variety of races throughout the year.

Professional Sports

Indianapolis is home to three professional sports teams and three minor league sports teams. Add to that events at the Indianapolis Motor Speedway and a variety of other events and championships, and you have a full professional sports schedule.

Indianapolis Colts

Indiana might consider itself home to basketball, but for the last several years the Indianapolis Colts have stolen Indianapolis's heart. Escaping from Baltimore in a famous nighttime move in 1984, the Colts became one of the premiere NFL teams.

Playing under the retractable roof of Lucas Oil Stadium, the Colts have made the playoffs 16 times since moving to Indianapolis, winning the conference championship twice and Super Bowl once. When you visit the stadium, be sure to check out the Colts Pro Shop inside the stadium. For a great picture opportunity inside the stadium, look out the large windows toward downtown. Outside the stadium, be sure to stop by the Peyton Manning statue.

When you go to a Colts game, you can easily walk to Lucas Oil Stadium from anywhere in downtown. In fact, the stadium is connected to the convention center by an underground walkway. It's not well-known, but you can go through security and enter the stadium with your tickets through this walkway. In fact, if your hotel or parking garage is connected by Indianapolis's large system of skywalks, then you can leave your coats and go to a Colts game without ever walking outside.

Indiana Pacers

Originally in the American Basketball Association before the merge, the Indiana Pacers play in the Eastern Conference of the NBA. Their best success came as three-time champions in the ABA, but they were conference champions in the NBA in 2000.

The Pacers play in Bankers Life Fieldhouse, another indoor stadium in downtown Indianapolis. Although it is not connected to hotels by skywalks, the stadium is very close to anywhere in downtown. The stadium sits at one end of Georgia St., a downtown street that is pedestrian friendly and is the site of many outdoor festivals throughout the year. If you drive to Bankers Life Fieldhouse, there is a parking garage on the east side of the stadium that is connected to the stadium, allowing you to avoid going outside.

When watching the Pacers, be sure to visit the Pacers Team Store. It is open both on game days and non-game days. When the Pacers aren't in town, Bankers Life Fieldhouse is probably still hosting events. From the home of the Indiana Fever, to concerts, shows, and other sporting events, Bankers Life Fieldhouse is a premiere and busy venue.

Indiana Fever

Also playing in Bankers Life Fieldhouse, the Indiana Fever is a team in the WNBA. More affordable and more recently successful than the Pacers, the Fever have qualified for the playoffs 13 out of their 17 years and have made the WNBA Finals twice, winning in 2012.

The Fever regularly ranks in the top half of WNBA teams in attendance. When watching a game, visit the Pacers Team Store in the stadium for Fever gear and souvenirs.

Other Professional Events

In addition to Indy's professional sports teams other professional sports visit Indianapolis either on a regular basis or from time to time. The PGA and LPGA often make stops in Indianapolis. Indy has hosted national gymnastics meets and professional figure skating events. And if professional wrestling is your thing, Indy also occasionally hosts the WWE.

Minor League Sports

Indianapolis is home to three minor league sports teams: the Indianapolis Indians, Indy Eleven, and Indy Fuel.

The **Indianapolis Indians** are a AAA baseball team affiliated with the Pittsburgh Pirates. Playing in Victory Field in downtown, the Indians are the second-oldest minor league team in the United States. A member of the International League, the Indians field a team of future MLB players, and occasionally a current MLB player either reassigned to AAA or on a rehabilitation assignment.

Victory Field is a great place to watch a baseball game. You can purchase tickets for seats in the stands, or you can purchase lawn tickets and sit in the grass just beyond the homerun wall. A fan favorite, sitting in the grass allows kids to run around and even permits you to bring your own food and drinks into the stadium (as long as you keep them in the grass).

The **Indy Eleven** is Indianapolis's soccer team that plays in the North American Soccer League. The team is only a few years old and has become wildly popular, far exceeding the attendance of other teams in the NASL.

Starting in 2018 the Indy Eleven play in Lucas Oil Stadium downtown (where the Colts play). Given the team's popularity, the Indy Eleven hope to build their own stadium in Indianapolis and even have their sights set on one day joining Major League Soccer.

The third minor league team in Indianapolis is the **Indy Fuel**. A newer member of the ECHL, the Indy Fuel is affiliated with NHL's Chicago Blackhawks.

Playing in Indiana Farmer's Coliseum at the Indiana State Fairgrounds, the Fuel continue a long history of minor league hockey in Indianapolis. Getting to a Fuel game from downtown is not difficult; it is only about a 15-minute drive from downtown.

Collegiate Sports

Butler

Located 15 minutes north of downtown Indy, Butler University is a private university of about 4,000 undergraduates. The Butler University Bulldogs compete in the Big East conference and have had success in basketball, soccer, volleyball, lacrosse, cross country and baseball.

Butler is probably best known for its men's basketball team – often making the NCAA tournament and having finished national runner-up two years in a row (2010 and 2011). Butler basketball plays in the historic Hinkle Fieldhouse – the sixth-oldest collegiate basketball arena still in use and the once-largest basketball arena in the United States (1928-1950). Hinkle Fieldhouse also used to host the Indiana high school basketball championships and was the arena used for the championship game in the movie *Hoosiers*.

IUPUI

Adjacent to downtown Indy, IUPUI (Indiana University-Purdue University Indianapolis) is primarily an Indiana University campus that offers some Purdue University programs. The IUPUI Jaguars compete in the Horizon League (Division I) and has had success in soccer, golf, and tennis.

The IUPUI campus is home to two stadiums that reach beyond their local collegiate duties. IUPUI's track and field stadium, the Michael A. Carroll Track & Soccer Stadium, hosted the Pan-American Games in 1987, the U.S. Olympic trials in 1988, collegiate championships, and the Indy Eleven soccer team (until they moved to Lucas Oil Stadium in 2018). The Indiana University Natatorium has hosted national championships and Olympic trials.

It is worth noting that the IUPUI men's and women's basketball teams play in Indiana Farmers Coliseum at the Indiana State Fairgrounds (not connected to IUPUI's campus).

Other Universities

Serving over 2,000 undergraduates, Marian University is a private, Catholic university, located about 10 minutes northwest of downtown Indianapolis. The Marian University Knights (NAIA) are best known for their collegiate cycling program. Competing at the Indy Cycloplex on campus, the Knights have won numerous national cycling championships and the Indy Cycloplex has hosted numerus championship meets.

The University of Indianapolis (6,000 undergraduates) is located about 10 minutes south of downtown Indy and competes in the NAIA.

Championships, Etc.

Several collegiate championship games and tournaments have been held in Indianapolis. IUPUI and Marian University have hosted a variety of collegiate championships and Olympic trials. Bankers Life Fieldhouse and Lucas Oil Stadium host a variety of basketball and football championships. And, coming up soon, Indy will host the NCAA men's Basketball Final Four in 2021 and the NCAA College Football Playoff championship game in 2022.

Stadium Tours

Lucas Oil Stadium (Colts and Indy Eleven)

*90 minutes
*playing field, locker room, press box, and more
*Monday-Friday, typically three times per day
*Separate prices for adults, seniors, and children (3 and under free)
*Book in advance or at window if available

Bankers Life Fieldhouse (Pacers and Fever)

groups of 15 or more only! – appointment only
*30-45 minutes
*Monday, Wednesday, Friday, two times per day
*Admission prices for adults, teachers, seniors, students, and children (4 and under free)
*must fill out a form online to book

Victory Field (Indiana)

groups only! – appointment only
*60 minutes
*playing field, seating area, grounds area, clubhouse, batting cages, and more
*April-September, Tuesday and Thursday on days of no home game, two times per day
*Admission prices are the same for everyone (except free admission for teachers and bus drivers)

Events, Concerts, Parks, and Conventions

Family Fun

While there are plenty of museums, spectator sports, and arts opportunities to enjoy with your family, you might be interested in a break. Here is a list of family-friendly attractions that both you and your kids will enjoy.

Zip Lining and More

Go Ape (Indianapolis – Eagle Creek Park) – tree top ropes course and zip lining
Zip City (Indianapolis – south) – indoor zip lining, rock climbing, ropes course, trampolines, and more
Edge Adventure Parks (Noblesville)

Rock Climbing

The Crux (Indianapolis – northwest)
Epic Climbing and Fitness (Indianapolis – west)
Climb Time (Fishers)
Hoosier Heights (Carmel)

Bowling

Woodland Bowling Center (Indianapolis – north)
Pinheads (Fishers)
Three-Two-Fun! (Noblesville)

Miniature Golf

Glow Golf (downtown – Circle Centre Mall)
Glow Golf (Indianapolis – north)

Pirate's Quest (Indianapolis – north)
Greatimes Family Fun Park (Indianapolis – south)
Monster Mini Golf (Avon)

Other

Top Golf (Fishers) – competitive golf games for any age, any skill, and during any weather

Boating

Canal (downtown): paddle boats
Eagle Creek Reservoir (Indianapolis – northwest): kayaks, canoes, standup paddleboards, paddle boats, pontoons, and sailboats
Geist Reservoir (Fishers): pontoons and kayaks
Morse Reservoir (Noblesville): pontoons

Concert and Theatre Locations

Ruoff Home Mortgage Music Center

Just a 25-30 minute drive northeast of downtown, the Ruoff Home Mortgage Music Center (formerly Klipsch Music Center) is an outdoor amphitheater that holds nearly 25,000 people. Ruoff Home Mortgage Music Center hosts a number of big concerts throughout the warmer months. In fact, Ruoff Home Mortgage Music Center often ranks towards the top of national lists for best amphitheater and yearly attendance numbers.

The Lawn at White River State Park

Located downtown and with room for over 50,000 people, The Lawn at White River State Park is the second of two major outdoor concert locations in the Indianapolis metro area. Like Ruoff Home Mortgage Music Center, The Lawn has also received accolades as a top outdoor concert venue. While its capacity is bigger, it tends to not attract the same big names that go to Ruoff. There is parking in both the state park and in downtown parking garages, but it is easily walkable from any downtown hotel.

Bankers Life Fieldhouse

The home of the Pacers and Fever also serves as Indianapolis's premier indoor concert location. Bankers Life Fieldhouse can seat up to 18,000 and might have a basketball game one night, a major concert the next night, and Disney on Ice the following night. Like The Lawn at White River State Park, Bankers Life Fieldhouse is located downtown and walkable from any downtown hotel.

The Old National Centre

The Old National Centre is more or less downtown, though perhaps not easily walkable from most downtown hotels. Located on trendy Massachusetts Ave., the Old National Centre has a theatre that seats 2,500, a separate concert hall, and a handful of other large areas that can host performances. The Old National Centre hosts some of Indianapolis's traveling Broadway shows, as well as plays, singers, and bands.

Hilbert Circle Theatre

Located downtown on the circle, the Hilbert Circle Theatre is home to the Indianapolis Symphony Orchestra. With seating for over 1,600 people, the theatre was also the host of Jimmy Fallon's Late Night during the Super Bowl in 2012.

Center for the Performing Arts

Located in suburban Carmel, the Center for the Performing Arts is a new arts complex with three different performing arts venues. The Palladium is the main theatre, seating 1,600 people. The Tarkington is a 500-seat theatre and The Studio Theater is a flexible room that seats just over 200. The Center for the Performing Arts is home for six resident dance, music, and theatre groups. The Center for the Performing Arts also has its own parking, cafe, and gift shop.

Other Theatres

Indianapolis and its suburbs house a number of other theatres that are used for plays, musicals, and dinner shows. The **Indiana Repertory Theatre** is located downtown and has two separate theatres. The **Metzger Building** (north part of downtown) began hosting The Cabaret in a new theatre in 2018. The **Phoenix Theatre** is located on trendy Massachusetts Ave. and hosts a variety of contemporary shows. Part of Butler University, **Clowes Memorial Hall**

39

hosts Broadway shows, concerts, plays, and other events. **Beef & Boards** is a dinner theatre located on the edge of Indianapolis, near Carmel and Zionsville.

Casinos

It's worth mentioning that two area casinos – Hoosier Park Racing & Casino in Anderson, Indiana and Indiana Grand Racing & Casino in Shelbyville, Indiana, both host a variety of concerts and shows throughout the year. Each casino is located 30-50 minutes outside of downtown.

Indiana State Fairgrounds & Event Center

More than just the host of the annual Indiana State Fair, the Indiana State Fairgrounds & Event Center holds more than 400 events each year, including concerts, sporting events, trade shows, and more. It even has a place you can ice skate! The Indiana State Fairgrounds & Event Center is only a 15-minute drive from downtown (public transportation is available).

Its main venues are the Indiana Farmers Coliseum – original home of the Indiana Pacers and current home of the Indy Fuel (hockey), the Hoosier Lottery Grandstand, and a large number of exposition halls and rooms.

Occurring every year in August, the **Indiana State Fair** hosts concerts, animal and agricultural competitions, rides, interactive exhibits, and a lot of deep-fried food. You can usually purchase advance tickets and most days of the fair are sponsored by a company or organization that might offer some type of discount.

Parking is easy at the fairgrounds. For most events, you can drive into the fairgrounds and park on one of their many lots. Keep in mind that your event building might be a decent walk from where you park. The fairgrounds offers shuttle buses during some events.

While there aren't hotels near the Indiana State Fairgrounds & Event Center, you can camp! The campground has full and partial-hookups for campers, allowing for year-round camping.

Parks and Outdoor Spaces

There are plenty of parks and outdoor spaces near downtown Indy. Indy's crown jewels are the **White River State Park** and the **Canal Walk**. Located on downtown's western edge, White River State Park is nestled between the White River and downtown. Offering green space, the admission-free park is home to outdoor concerts, surrey bike rentals, Segway tours, multiple museums, the Indianapolis Zoo, and is connected to the Canal Walk.

The 1.5-mile Canal Walk extends north from White River State Park and winds past museums and Indianapolis neighborhoods. A popular jogging spot, you can rent paddle boats and even take a gondola ride. You can rent surrey bikes in the adjacent White River State Park and ride them along the Canal Walk.

Adjacent to White River State Park and the Canal Walk, Indianapolis's **Military Park** hosts various festivals throughout the year.

Another outdoor area is a 5-block stretch of parks and memorials about one block north of Monument Circle. **University Park**, the **Indiana War Memorial**, and **Veteran's Memorial Plaza** make up the area. Be sure to read more about these areas on p 25.

While it might not have very much green, **Georgia St.** is another outdoor area in downtown Indy. While most of the time it functions as a two-way street with a large pedestrian median, Georgia St. is closed off during major events and becomes the hub of downtown celebrations. Georgia St. stretches from the Indianapolis Convention Center to Bankers Life Fieldhouse and even has an entrance to Circle Centre Mall.

Two other major areas outside of downtown Indy are **Eagle Creek Park** (Indianapolis – northwest) and **Fort Harrison State Park** (Lawrence). Both offer hiking, fishing, and golf. In addition, Eagle Creek is home to Go Ape (zip lines and rope course).

Major Conventions

With one of the 20 largest convention centers in the United States and the convention center being connected to more hotel rooms by skywalks than any other city in the United States, Indianapolis has a thriving convention industry. Here is a list of the major conventions that have been (or plan to be) visiting Indianapolis yearly and the approximate time of year they normally hold their convention.

(This list excludes local events.)

Convention/Event	Approximate Month	Approximate Attendance
JAMfest Super Nationals	January	25,000
Indiana ComicCon	March-April	30,000
American Coatings Show	April	10,000
FDIC International	April	30,000
Indy PopCon	June	40,000
Beachbody Coach Summit	June	25,000
GenCon	August	60,000
National FFA	October	60,000

Christmas in Indy

Several of the museums and attractions listed in this book pull out all the stops at Christmas. Here is a list of some of the special things you can experience.

Monument Circle – *Circle of Lights*: claiming to be the world's largest Christmas tree, Monument Circle is reimagined as a gigantic tree surrounded by toy soldiers. (free)

Indianapolis Zoo – *Christmas at the Zoo*: experience select zoo animals at dark along with thousands and thousands of lights all over the zoo. (admission required)

Eiteljorg Museum – *Jingle Rails*: nearly a quarter mile of model train track connects models of Indianapolis and points westward – including Las Vegas, Mt. Rushmore, and the Grand Canyon. (admission required)

Newfields – *Winter Lights*: a million lights adorn Newfields outdoor grounds where you can also roast s'mores and drink warm drinks. (admission required)

The Children's Museum – *Jolly Days Winter Wonderland*: a special area including a two-story "sledding" hill and a holiday children's play area. (admission required)

Indianapolis Motor Speedway – *Lights at the Brickyard*: a 2-mile drive-through light display. (admission required)

Reynolds Farm Equipment – a drive-through Christmas light display in Fishers at a John Deere retail store. (free)

PLANNING YOUR TRIP

Where to Stay

With over 22,000 hotel rooms in the metro area and more than 7,000 rooms located downtown, you have a ton of options for lodging in Indianapolis. Hotels include options like the 1,000+ rooms of the JW Marriott, the posh rooms of the Conrad, boutique hotels like the Alexander and Le Meridien, or less expensive name brand options.

Out of the 7,000 downtown rooms, over 4,000 are connected to the Indiana Convention Center by skywalk. Many have both self-parking and valet parking options. Some even offer a complimentary airport shuttle.

Staying outside of downtown increases the number of rooms available but doesn't necessarily increase they types of hotels available. Within the city limits, three main clusters of hotels are on the west side near the airport, on the east side including the conference hotel Indianapolis Marriott East, and on the north side including slightly higher quality (and more expensive) hotels near major shopping centers.

There are clusters of chain hotels in most suburbs, with slightly more expensive options in the northern suburbs. One advantage to staying outside of downtown is that most of these hotels offer free parking and some even offer free breakfast.

There are also bed and breakfast and house rental options scattered outside the immediate downtown area and throughout the metro area.

Where to Eat

The Indianapolis eating scene has received quite a bit of national recognition lately. With over 200 places to eat downtown, a handful of unique Indy neighborhoods, and more options in the suburbs, you can find just about anything to please everybody's palate and budget.

Favorites include fine dining at St. Elmo Steak House (downtown) or Ruth's Chris Steak House (downtown) and unique pizzas at Jockamo Pizza (Indianapolis – east). Downtown Indy has popular chain restaurants like Hard Rock Café and P.F. Chang's. If expensive dining isn't for your budget, then consider the downtown Steak 'n Shake and plenty of options in the food court at Circle Centre Mall.

Aside from downtown, Indianapolis has a handful of neighborhoods with unique dining options. Immediately southeast of downtown, Fletcher Place has Indy's renowned Milktooth and other restaurants. Immediately northeast of downtown, Massachusetts Ave. is overloaded with restaurants and nightspots. For a college-town experience, trek 15 minutes north of downtown to Broad Ripple for eclectic shops and dining options.

Outside of Indianapolis, Indy's suburbs contain a wide variety of national chain restaurants. For more unique dining choices, check out the Arts District in Carmel, the Historic Noblesville Square in Noblesville, and Main St. in Zionsville.

When to Go – Crowds and Weather

Crowds

One of the nice things about Indianapolis is that there always seem to be people downtown. That doesn't mean it is always crowded, but rather it always seems alive. It is usually easy to find parking and not too difficult to find a place to eat. Downtown hotel rooms do fill up during big events, but there are thousands of rooms available outside of downtown, most within a 30-minute drive.

Crowds don't necessarily change based on the time of year. The colder months bring people to Colts and Pacers games, while the warmer months bring people to Indians and Fever games, as well as outdoor areas like the Indianapolis Zoo and Canal Walk. Conferences and concerts occur year-round, however, so the time of year doesn't necessarily affect crowd size.

The best advice about crowds is to check for any major events or conventions. Conventions focused on high school or college students tend to make the downtown mall's food court extra busy. While some events such as parades and marathons close roads.

Weather

Located in the Midwest, Indianapolis truly experiences all four seasons of weather. In the summer, you can expect warm, humid days – with some very pleasant days and other very hot days. In the winter, you will typically get cold weather with the chance for rain or snow – with some days being bitterly cold and other days surprisingly decent.

While weather could always be a factor, keep in mind that downtown Indianapolis has many places that are connected by skywalks. In the event of snow, Indiana plows their main roads aggressively and they are rarely impassable. Speaking of snow, Indianapolis sees an average of 21 inches over about 4 months, and large snowfalls usually occur only a few times a year.

Getting There

Driving

Indiana calls itself the Crossroads of America and it's easy to see why. Seven different interstate highways travel through Indiana and four of them go through Indianapolis. Indianapolis is just a few hours from Chicago, St. Louis, Louisville, Cincinnati, Columbus, and Detroit.

But, while four interstates connect and then travel through Indianapolis, only two interstates actually travel through the middle of Indianapolis. If you take I-69 or I-74 to Indianapolis, you will have to take I-465 (Indy's loop) to either I-65 or I-70 to get downtown.

Once you're downtown, most roads travel directly east-west or north-south. Be aware that some roads are one-way roads, which most GPSs can easily manage. Downtown traffic is usually manageable but can be difficult right before and after a sporting or other major event. Watch lane markers carefully so you can be in the correct lane and plan your turns a couple of blocks in advance.

Flying

If you fly into Indianapolis, then you will fly into Indy's only international airport, the world-renowned Indianapolis International Airport. Consistently rated the best airport in North America, Indy's airport serves a large number of destinations and its wide concourses offer plenty of room to move, relax, shop, and dine while waiting on a flight.

Renting a car is easy, as eight different rental companies operate from the first floor of the parking garage – right across from where you collect your luggage. IndyGo (Indianapolis's bus system) offers regular bus service from the airport to downtown and other locations. If you're going downtown, check out IndyGo's Route 8, which provides a very affordable option to get downtown. There are also other bus operators who operate buses from the airport to other regional Indiana destinations.

In addition to renting a car or taking a bus, you can take a taxi, use Uber or Lyft, use BlueIndy (car sharing service), or hire a limousine. There are also a handful of airport-area hotels that offer free shuttles to and from the airport.

And if private flying is your thing, you have a few different options:

*Indy South Greenwood Airport (KHFY – Greenwood, Indiana) boasts the closest drive to downtown (aside from Indianapolis International) and a 5,100-ft runway.

*Indianapolis Regional Airport (KMQJ – Mt. Comfort, Indiana) offers access to Indianapolis from the east side and a 6,005-ft runway.

*Indianapolis Metropolitan Airport (KUMP – Fishers, Indiana) offers quick access to Interstate 69 and a 3,580-ft runway.

*Indianapolis Executive Airport (KTYQ – Zionsville, Indiana) offers quick access to Carmel, Zionsville, and Westfield and a 5,500-ft runway.

*Eagle Creek Airpark (KEYE – Indianapolis, Indiana) is located on the northwest side of Indy and has a 4,200-ft runway.

Trains

Amtrak offers the only regional rail service to Indianapolis. Amtrak offers daily service to and from Chicago (with a few destinations between). In addition, Amtrak offers service three days a week to and from New York City via Washington DC and Cincinnati, OH.

Buses

Greyhound, Megabus, and Hoosier Ride! offer regional service to Indianapolis. Greyhound has a station in downtown and offers multiple routes several times a day to destinations across the United States. Megabus uses a downtown IndyGo bus stop as its local stop and offers a limited number of out-of-state destinations. Hoosier Ride! is run by a local bus company, Miller Transportation, and offers routes to most cities and major towns in Indiana, as well as some locations in Tennessee, Kentucky, Ohio, Michigan, and Illinois.

Getting Around While There

One of the biggest surprises of visitors to Indianapolis is how **walkable** downtown is. Within a small, compact area, you can walk to three sports stadiums, a half-dozen cultural institutions, a major mall, the convention center, thousands of hotel rooms and hundreds of restaurants. If you are staying downtown and your destinations are downtown, then you do not need a car and you won't need to use public transportation.

If you need to go outside of downtown, then you can use **public transportation**. Unfortunately, Indianapolis doesn't have light rail, so public transportation is limited to IndyGo, Indianapolis's bus system. The Indy metro is in the process of constructing dedicated rapid bus service, which means regular service for buses traveling in dedicated travel lines. It will be kind of like a train, but without tracks.

Of course you can always **drive a car**. With so many interstate highways, it is easy to get just about anywhere in the metro area in a half hour or less. Indiana has worked hard to ease traffic on its highways and with the exception of a few bottlenecks during rush hour, you should be able to drive most places without much trouble. Like most Midwestern cities, Indianapolis's infrastructure is built around the automobile, so that means you should be able to find ample parking wherever you go.

Besides the normal options of **taxis**, **Uber** and **Lyft**, Indianapolis also boasts **bicycle sharing** and **car sharing**. The **Indiana Pacers Bikeshare** has 25 stations located downtown and extending slightly away from downtown. **BlueIndy** offers car sharing throughout downtown and points beyond. BlueIndy uses electric cars that can seat up to four adults. Riders purchase membership fees for each of these two services and then pay for each use.

Indy's Suburbs

Like most Midwestern cities, Indianapolis's suburbs consist of an inner ring of older suburbs and an outer ring of newer suburbs. Since Indianapolis consolidated into a city-county government in 1970, many of its inner ring suburbs are now part of the city of Indianapolis.

In fact, only four municipalities in Marion County are not a part of Indianapolis – Beech Grove and Speedway (located mostly inside of I-465) and Lawrence and Southport (located mostly outside of I-465).

Indianapolis's outer ring of suburbs includes:

Greenwood (south)

Plainfield, Avon, and Brownsburg (west)

Zionsville, Carmel, Westfield, Fishers, and Noblesville (north)

Carmel, Westfield, Fishers, and Noblesville are in Hamilton County, which was named by Forbes.com as America's Best Place to Raise a Family in 2008. Similar accolades have gone to Carmel and Fishers – each snagging #1 rankings in the U.S. for best places to live in various magazines.

Indianapolis's suburbs provide varied shopping, dining, and lodging opportunities. You can find Indy's only IKEA and Top Golf in Fishers, as well as Cabella's in Noblesville. Noblesville and Zionsville boast scenic downtowns with shops and restaurants, while Carmel is truly a city unto itself, with fine dining, high-end retail, and a vibrant arts scene.

Not to be outdone by their northern neighbors, Plainfield boasts an outdoor mall and family water park, while Greenwood has a large indoor mall.

Shopping

Indianapolis has a variety of shopping experiences – including major malls, local shops, and suburban downtowns.

As for malls, **Circle Centre Mall** is conveniently located in downtown Indy. You can easily walk to it from anywhere downtown and it is even connected to the city's skywalk system. (In fact, you might have to walk through the mall to go from one section of the skywalk to another.) Circle Centre Mall, which is planning to undergo a multi-million dollar upgrade, contains normal mall stores, a decent-sized food court, sit-down restaurants, a movie theater and an interactive game area.

Located in northern Indianapolis, **Castleton Square** is the largest indoor mall in Indiana. It contains normal mall stores and is anchored by a large number of department stores. **The Fashion Mall at Keystone** is also located in northern Indianapolis (just a few miles from Castleton Square) and contains many upper-end stores including the Apple Store, Crate and Barrel, Pottery Barn, and Saks Fifth Avenue. These two malls in northern Indy are connected by 82nd St./86th St. (the same road – it's weird). Along this street are a lot more stores and restaurants.

Other major malls include indoor **Greenwood Park Mall** (Greenwood), and outdoor malls: **Hamilton Town Center** (Noblesville), **Clay Terrace** (Carmel) and **The Shops at Perry Crossing** (Plainfield).

Aside from malls, Indy has some neat neighborhoods and suburban downtowns. Broad Ripple is an eclectic neighborhood in northern Indy. Massachusetts Ave (just barely northeast of downtown) is a trendy nightspot with shopping and dining. Fountain Square (just barely southeast of downtown) is gaining popularity as a retail and dining destination.

In the suburbs, both Zionsville and Noblesville have quaint downtowns with antique shops and dining. Carmel's downtown has a contemporary mix of high-end boutiques, dining, and other retail.

In addition to malls, eclectic shops, and antiques, Indianapolis also has an IKEA in Fishers, a Cabella's in Noblesville and three Costcos.

Day Trips Outside Indianapolis

Conner Prairie

Conner Prairie is a living history museum in Fishers (25-30 minutes northeast of downtown Indy) that shows what life was like in the 1800s. A Smithsonian Affiliate, Conner Prairie is massive and houses a main museum building, an entire town based in 1836, an interactive Civil War village, an Indian camp, the original William Conner house, a 4-story interactive treehouse, a hot air balloon ride, animal encounters, and more.

Children and adults will appreciate interacting with employees who dress and act their parts. You can learn how to create 19th century crafts and use 19th century tools.

Conner Prairie is open year-round, though most areas are closed during the coldest months. As such, admission prices vary based on the time of year and there are separate prices for adults, children, and seniors. Hot air balloon rides cost extra and Conner Prairie offers free admission for military members and discounts for their family.

Conner Prairie has a gift shop and a cafeteria, as well as free parking.

Hoosier Gym

Located in Knightstown (about 45 minutes east of downtown Indy), Hoosier Gym is the main gym where the movie *Hoosiers* (1986) was filmed. Starring Gene Hackman, *Hoosiers* is a basketball movie that tells the true story of the 1954 Milan High School basketball team that unexpectedly won the state basketball championship.

Hoosier Gym was originally Knightstown High School's gym and was restored for the movie. Tours are free and generally offered seven days a week. However, you should call in advance as the gym frequently hosts private events and basketball games. As part of the tour, you will see the gym and the locker room. You can even take some shots on the gym floor. Renting the gym is very affordable – you can rent it for parties or events and have full access to playing basketball as well.

There is a small gift shop and museum located in the entrance of the gym. There are restrooms, but no cafeteria. Parking is free on the street.

Brown County

Nicknamed the "Little Smokies" after Smoky Mountain National Park, Brown County is home to hills and woods, an eclectic town, and Brown County State Park. Located about an hour south of downtown Indy, Brown County represents quite an escape from the flat cornfields of central Indiana.

Brown County State Park is the focal point of the area. It is Indiana's largest state park and includes winding roads, campgrounds, hiking, horse trails, mountain bike trails, and the Abe Martin Lodge. The lodge has both hotel rooms and cabins, as well as a small indoor water park and conference space.

Nashville, Indiana sits at the northeast entrance to Brown County State Park and is home to quaint shops, restaurants, and hotels. You might spend an entire day visiting Nashville's shops and galleries. The greater Brown County area hosts numerous cabins you can rent as well as outdoor activities such as zip lining, horseback riding, and mountain biking. Just a few miles north of Nashville is Bean Blossom, Indiana, which is home to the Bill Monroe Music Park and

Campground. (Bill Monroe is considered the father of bluegrass music.)

Major Universities

While Indianapolis is home to a few colleges and universities, most of Indiana's well-known universities are located outside of Indy. **Indiana University** is located in Bloomington (near Brown County) and is about an hour south of Indianapolis. **Purdue University** is located in West Lafayette and is about an hour northwest of Indianapolis. **Ball State University** is located in Muncie and is about an hour northeast of Indianapolis. **Indiana State University** is located in Terre Haute and is about an hour west of Indianapolis. The **University of Notre Dame** is located in South Bend and is about 2 ½ hours north of Indianapolis.

Everything Else

Other Resources

Remember, this is just an introduction to Indianapolis. Here are some resources that might help you plan your trip.

Websites

www.visitindy.com – the best website to learn more about upcoming events, to find specific types of restaurants and lodging, and to find current deals.

www.indystar.com – Indy's daily newspaper that contains a "Things to Do" section with articles about events, attractions, and restaurants

www.downtownindy.org – focuses on downtown: living there and visiting there

www.icclos.com – Indiana Convention Center website

www.ibj.com – Indianapolis Business Journal

Books

100 Things to Do in Indianapolis Before You Die (Ashley Petry, 2014)

Indianapolis, IN: A Photographic Portrait (Jason Lavengood and Shari Held, 2017)

Indianapolis Colts: The Complete Illustrated History (Lew Freedman, 2013)

Best Hikes Near Indianapolis (Nick Werner, 2012)

Indianapolis Restaurant Guide 2018 (Jonathan M. Briand, 2017)

*Visit **www.shortandsweetintroductions.com/indylinks** for links to all of these resources, plus links to attraction websites.*

Visit *www.shortandsweetintroductions.com/indylinks* for websites and resources

Did you enjoy this book? If so, then please leave a review wherever you purchased it!

Do you have any questions, comments, or suggestions? Contact me at *shortandsweetintroductions.com/contact*

Would you like free previews and updates about future books? Join my email list at *shortandsweetintroductions.com/email*

About the Author

My name is Joe Dodridge and I live in Fishers, Indiana. My full-time job is a high school teacher. I'm also the pastor of a small, new church. I'm married and we have two children.

I write both travel books and Christian devotionals.

My writing "career" really started in eleventh grade when I wrote that year's first essay for English. My teacher gave me my rough draft back with over half of it crossed out and told me what I wrote was useless. I went on to get a C on that first paper and it was the beginning of a brutal boot camp experience of learning how to properly write. (split infinitive – it's OK!)

After countless papers in college and graduate school, my graduate thesis advisor was the daughter of an English professor and a journal editor. So, I went through boot camp 2.0.

In 2007, I started writing a daily devotional online. I bought a website and wrote over 150 devotionals.

Since then, I've written a lot of things that haven't made it out of my computer until July 2017 when I wrote my first book, *A Short and Sweet Introduction to Walt Disney World Resort: 2017-2018*. That book came out of my love for Disney World, my love for travel, and my desire to finally get a book written.

Then, I added *Our Kids - Our Responsibility, Months 1-3 "Jesus's Teaching," 250 Tips and Tricks for Walt Disney World Resort*, and the newest edition of *A Short and Sweet Introduction to Walt Disney World Resort: 2018*.

Other Books by Joe Dodridge

250 Tips and Tricks for Walt Disney World Resort (January 2018)

The problem with most tips books is they aren't full of that many tips. This book gives you over 250 tips – no stories about tips, just tips.

Our Kids – Our Responsibility, Months 1-6 "Jesus's Teaching" and *"Genesis"* (January, March 2018)

If you're like our family, you've tried daily devotions and failed. This weekly family devotional goes more in-depth and provides an extra time just for parents.

A Short and Sweet Introduction to Walt Disney World Resort: 2018 (February 2018)

Most Disney World guide books read like encyclopedias – too much information and not enough introduction. This second edition, 60-page guide book introduces you to the parks, hotels, dining, and more without overwhelming you!

Future Book Projects

A Disney World Combo Book! – A Short and Sweet Introduction to Walt Disney World Resort AND 250 Tips and Tricks for Walt Disney World Resort

Our Kids – Our Responsibility, Months 7-12

A Short and Sweet Introduction to Washington DC

Just For You...

 Join my email list for book updates at shortandsweetintroductions.com/email

 Share this book on Facebook, Twitter, or Instagram.

Printed in December 2021
by Rotomail Italia S.p.A., Vignate (MI) - Italy